Deprived Truth, Deprived Identity

Mignon Valliere Walker

Dedication

I would like to dedicate this book to all individuals, young and old, who have experienced life events that has mentally and emotionally stuck with them up through adulthood and is searching for or have achieved a breakthrough. May God bless you.

Acknowledgements

I would like to thank my husband, Adam, for his unconditional love, undying support and encouragement. Thank you for being all of my missing pieces.

Sincerest thanks to my children, Janaevia, Jamohri, Jachin and Javari for their love and understanding. I wouldn't be me without you.

Mignon Valliere Walker

There are so many of people who live their lives trusting and believing in what is their truth, their self-being. But, what if your truth is not really yours? What do you do when you believe you have been completely betrayed by unconditional love? What do you do when opportunities, for that person to make it right with you, come and go without any action taken place? What do you do when unconditional love finally apologizes after countless years (but not on their own accord; more like forced)? Is your heart open to receive? Do you feel as if there is nothing you can do but to accept their apology to include an incomplete explanation or understanding? What do you do when your unconditional love is your parent, whom you love and trust?

As long as I can remember, I had been told one thing all my life to find out that specific things weren't truth; yet, the real truth was always in my face. There wasn't anyone brave enough to stand their ground and let me know of the truth; instead, for 30+ years, I lived my life blind with complete vision while everyone else (my family) watched.

The story you are about to read is my recollection of how I recall the chronological events that happened within my life while on a journey to 'find and bond with my paternal family'.

I recall many different meaningful things in life. But, the one meaningful event I recall was to not have my biological father within my life and not have a reason as to why. Growing up, I really didn't press in trying to find out details of why he (my biological father) was not present in my life. Asking a grown-up 'adult questions' just wasn't what you did as a child, well, my childhood. From time to time, when the opportunity presented itself, I would ask specific question(s) and I would be given an answer, cut and dry with no explanation. Now, when it is your parent that is giving you the information, as a child, you tend to believe them, as what I did, and that was that. Truthfully, there was no reason for me, as a child, to think otherwise.

There are many ways I can begin to tell my story. As you read along, please know that when I quote a year of age, this is only from what I can remember and what I believe my age was at that time. Well, let me begin.

I have one sister and two brothers from the same mother. These are the siblings I grew up with. Between us, we had the same mother, same home training, same discipline, same love, same fun, same joy and same childhood (to the extent of being a girl or a boy). To one, there wasn't anything missing, right?

Well, one of my brothers is the eldest before me and we do not share the same biological father. I am second to oldest (the next child) and then I have a sister, after me, and a younger brother, whom is after my sister, in which they share of the same biological father. For the most part, we had a happy childhood; moved around a bit much, but my childhood overall was good—I can honestly say that.

My mom was a stickler for discipline. She would sometimes talk to us using only facial expressions. And I'll tell you, whippings were the worse--not in an abusive way, we just didn't enjoy getting a spanking. I mean, what child likes getting a spanking of any kind? She always made sure we got the picture and we understood the reasoning of getting spanked; prior, during and after the spanking. Meaning, she explained herself the entire time and for each child she spanked. It's almost funny when I now think about it. She cared, loved and did everything and anything in her power to protect us. She didn't let anyone mess with us and believe me, no one, and I do mean no one, ever did. My mother is a black, strong woman, independent, prideful, stubborn and at times she can be mean with her words and facial expressions as if you messed with her in the wrong way. She TOOK CARE of us, seriously. I don't recall not having a roof over my head, clean clothes on my back, hair combed and food to eat. We always looked good and presentable.

I can remember as a child, I was such a neat freak who had to have everything in its order. My toys were put away neatly and my clothes were always pressed neatly and matching (coordinated). I even matched my underwear and socks to the outfit I was wearing. When I became older (adolescent), I recall I used to iron my socks and underwear—I just had to be neat. I guess, I had to have gotten those habits from my mother. When I look back at all my baby photos, there was never a hair out of place or my wardrobe off-key. I have pictures to prove this, well, my mom does. But, I say all this because this will always be my mother, I love her dearly and I have the utmost respect for her even though what I am about to tell you may have you all thinking otherwise. C'mon, she is my mother!

Here we go!

Growing up at the approximate age of three or four, I recall calling my younger siblings' father, "Daddy". He was the one that was present in our lives. In my eyes and in my mind, I thought he was my daddy. As a young child, if no one tells you differently, you don't think anything otherwise. He was around; my siblings called him daddy, and I thought he must be my daddy too. He had to be my daddy as well, he was always around and I was born before my siblings. We all went places together, we attended family events.

During Easter time, I remember we used to go to my younger siblings grandmother's (which is whom I thought was my grandmother at the time as well) double-wide trailer. Her trailer had a full front deck porch and she used to have the biggest and the best Easter Egg

Hunts. She was the coolest. She had diamond rings on almost every finger and her nickname was "Diamond Rose". We called her "Mawmaw Rose". She had all the really nice stuff a home could have. She even had one of the first wide screen television where there were three colored lights (green, red, blue—I believe) that projected the picture onto her screen and she also had satellite (like the ones in the late 1970s). Whenever we would visit, she would say, "go look in the freezer"; and to my surprise, ice cream, popsicles galore. This was kid heaven. Talk about, that was the life. I'll tell you, I thought she was the coolest and she was always nice to all of us. No differences. I always enjoyed going to see her.

We also used to live in the country on a farm in a trailer behind my younger siblings' grandfather (which is whom I thought was my grandfather at the time as well). Their grandparents didn't live together, but they were still married I believe. Hey, trailer homes were popular back then and we had fun all the time. Besides, I didn't worry about where we lived; I just know we always had a roof over our heads. There was so much land to run around and we had fun with the animals. When I say farm, I mean farm. They processed their own goat milk, made their own sausage, slaughtered their own hogs, had chickens, roosters, ducks, geese, horses, cows and lots and lots of trees and land.

I remember one time my older brother and I would flip circles around the wood pole that held our clothes in the closet. We would climb the wall with our feet and flip over the wood pole. On this particular morning, the wood pole broke while one of was flipping (I think it was my turn at the time). Of course, there was a loud bang, crash, and a hard thud from hitting the floor. My brother and I just looked at each other and prayed that our mother didn't hear it. Their room was literally on the other end of the trailer home. We first, quickly fixed the wood pole and then we just sat there, hoping and pleading to ourselves and watching the bedroom door. Well, of course, our mother has ears of a wolf, and she comes in with the belt because she just knew we had done something wrong. I don't recall us getting a whipping, just being fussed at for being too loud and that was that. I believe because it was real early in the morning and she was still somewhat sleep/tired. Fun times!

I also remember my parents used to drive a light brown or tan-like vehicle, could have been a Nova (something like it), and at times when we went places (locally) I used to lay on the platform that was behind the backseats right under the back windshield. I used to lay there and watch the sky and the clouds. That was so much fun and peaceful to me and I never understood exactly why I used to do it. That was like my thing, none of my other siblings did this and my mother allowed me to do it. Could be, my siblings just didn't care to do it. Today, that would be considered dangerous for children to do. Fun times!

Well, I get a little older (maybe a year older) and my mother and he (younger siblings' father) I guess are no longer a couple. Now as a child, I am not necessarily aware of that; but, I do remember that he was not around as much. It was noticeable, but not necessarily of an importance to us as kids (from my point of view); we just kept doing childlike stuff and didn't really pay it any mind.

Now at this time, I recall we are visiting and going to my maternal grandparents a bit much. My grandmother lived in the city. I remember spending so much time there. Fun times too! Listen, I remember climbing the huge fig trees in her backyard all the way to the top. My grandmother used to canned figs and I can't tell you how many fig sandwiches I have eaten, and she didn't mind one bit. We used to play hide-and-go-seek in the house, outside of the house; freeze-tag in the house and outside of the house. She just had one of those houses where you can run around, dig around and find interesting stuff. And by all means, she kept everything neat and in order. That's how she always knew when we had been in her things, digging. We would always think, 'How did she know?'

On some occasions, when my older brother and I knew beforehand that our grandmother was about to leave the house to make an errand and she wouldn't allow us to go, we used to go hide in her car on the backseat floor and wait until she would drive down the street before we would pop up from the backseat. She would always say, "Y'all kids scared the sh*t out of me" and then she would laugh cause she knew how much we just wanted to tag along with her. My brother and I would always be surprised to hear her say a cuss (curse) word because I don't necessarily remember her being an avid curser. I could tell she really didn't mind us coming along, but I don't think she enjoyed us scaring her. Our little scheme worked every time, so of course she just started letting us go with her. My maternal grandmother's house was like the 'go-to' house for family gatherings or when family came in town to visit. So, you can imagine just how much fun times and memories were captured there.

Again, we moved around a lot and that wasn't so bad for me. From a child's point of view and me reflecting back, I can recall every place we lived our living conditions were good.

Moving on.

I guess I am now about the age of five or six and I remember one of our older female cousins taking us (me and my siblings) to the community pool. My older cousin was first cousins with my mother and second cousins to us. Well, up to this point in time, I thought my daddy and biological father was the same father as my younger siblings'. I can't remember if I had asked my mother previously about any daddy situation. I didn't have a reason to. The community pool was in walking distance from where we currently lived and therefore, we made our way there by feet. So, we're at the community pool and a few minutes after we arrive, my cousin spots my daddy and then proceeds to ask me if I wanted to meet him, which was sort of confusing to me, because I already know my daddy (whom I am thinking is the same man as my siblings). So to not be defiant, I said yes. Not thinking if it was anyone different. So, my cousin and I proceed to go and meet him and my cousin tells me 'This is your daddy'. At the time, it was confusing but not confusing because at that age I really didn't pay it any mind, I was more concerned with having fun at the pool than anything. I was so proud of myself and felt a bit independent because I used my own monies and paid 75 cents to access the pool. I remember walking tall with my three quarters in hand, ready to pay the attendant and enter the facilities. So of course, I wanted to get my money's worth and not waste any time not having fun. As I think about it, as we were all standing there, I do remember staring at him as if to say "you look different" and he, "the new daddy", just looking right back at me, smiling and caressing my face. Then, he picked me up, and began hugging and kissing me. I felt safe because my cousin was right there beside me and she was a person not to mess with. He appeared to be surprised and very excited to see me. He then asked me if I wanted to go swimming with him and I replied, yes. So to make my day even better with me feeling all 'big girl' and independent, I got the chance to swim in (as what I called it) the 'big people' pool with him. He and I positioned me on his back and we swam around a bit. All of a sudden, everyone had to immediately get out of the pool because someone had had a bowel movement in the pool (if I am not mistaken). I believe at this time, I went back to the kiddie pool. In the process of him escorting me back to the kiddie pool, he had located my cousin and it appeared they both began conversing, but it was brief. Overall, it appeared he was happy to see me and that made me happy inside and I felt special. Time passed and we then leave the community pool and proceed to go home. As I walked all the way home, all I could think about was that I had another daddy and that my other daddy wasn't my daddy. Those thoughts went through my mind over and over again. So, I believe I asked my cousin if he really was my daddy and she replied, "Yes, that is your real daddy."

I believe my cousin may have been living with us at the time or it could be she was just around a lot. We had so much fun with her. You know, I believe she may have taught me how to iron my clothes. I believed she helped my mother out a lot as well (well I assume). Talk about she was so much FUN. She used to help get us (my siblings and I) out of whippings, talk about she was GREAT! I wasn't friends (too fond of) with spankings, so imagine how thrilled I was of having my cousin there and helping us out of kid troubles.

Oh my gosh! I just remembered something and you all may think I am weird. At that time, I used to LOVE to eat just plain BUTTER! No, not a whole stick of butter. My mom used to buy the sticks of butter (they didn't have the tubs or bowls of butter as they do now). And she would have the stick of butter in its butter container sitting on the door of the refrigerator. I would sneak (all the time) going to the refrigerator and just scooping some butter with my index finger. I used to leave these small, little finger-scooped marks in the butter and she knew it was me because I was the only one (sibling) doing that. I apologize for jumping off subject; I just remember butter tastes so good and I used to always get yelled at for leaving finger markings in the butter, let alone eating butter.

Ok. I'm back.

Well, when we arrived home from the community pool, I remember my cousin calling out to my mother to see where she was located within the house. I also recall my cousin telling my mother that she had seen my father (whom they (all family members) were told was my father though unknowing to me) and that she had introduced us. I assumed it wasn't like it was a secret so my cousin wasn't necessarily soft spoken while talking about it ('cause I heard the conversation while sitting in my room, quiet as a mouse, eaves dropping...well trying to). I remember my mother yelling, "What?!" She said it so loud, she scared me. My toys and I just sat there frozen stiff as a nail listening to make sure she wasn't yelling at me. A few seconds later, my mom and my cousin began to argue. Whew, I was just glad that she wasn't yelling at me or for me.

Their argument wasn't a huge, loud argument, but I recall them both exchanging words back and forth. It appeared my cousin was shocked that my mother would be upset about the whole thing. I really couldn't understand why my mother would not have approved of my cousin letting me meet my father. I really couldn't understand why that would make her mad and angry. That was very puzzling to me; although, I really don't know exactly what was said among their conversation per say and what words were exactly exchanged, but even so, for my mother to get upset about it was confusing to me. Of course, I asked no questions and did not speak of it.

You may be wondering why I didn't say anything. Well first, after seeing how my mother became mad and angry at my cousin and second, I remembered that children did not address adults with adult stuff, so, I decided that I for sure wasn't trying to risk it thus getting fussed at and/or even a whippin'. Uh-uh, not me. Then my cousin was not around as much and I assumed she was no longer living with us, but she would still come around. I say that because she just wasn't constantly there with us on a consistent basis; like sleep overs and dining with us. I think within a short timeframe after all of this happened, my mother eventually sat me down and then told me that the man at the community pool was really my father. I remember sitting there thinking that he really was my daddy. I didn't ask any question to what she told me, what she said is what she said. And that was that. I went back to playing with my Barbie dolls, my Legos, my Transformers, He-Man and Battlecat.

So now, this new father is in my life. I am so excited because I am like, I have a NEW daddy and to think he is all mine alone. As a child, that's what I was thinking. Now of course, we have moved since then in a duplex apartment or townhouse (if that makes sense). This 'new dad' decides he wants to spend time with me. I assumed this because one day, out-of-the-blue, he shows up to our home. I remember my siblings and I peeked from the small hallway to see who the person was at the door. I personally had remembered his face and I whispered to my siblings that I think it was my daddy and so, we all went back to our rooms to play, quickly and quietly. We didn't want to get caught snooping and risk getting fussed at and/or a whippin'. When we returned back to our rooms, I could tell they were like puzzled a bit, but didn't really think much of it. I think my younger siblings' thought their father was my older brother and I father as well. I mean so did I. I am unsure of what my older brother thought. They didn't ask me any questions either as I am sure they knew I had just as much information as they did.

I assumed he (my new daddy) and my mother talked and I remember my mother calling me from the room and telling me that I was going to spend some time with him that day. I was too thrilled and so excited that I ran back to my room grabbed my shoes, told my siblings I was leaving and ran back to the living room and proceeded to go with him. While waiting to leave, all I could do is stare at him. He was so tall like a bean stalk with the biggest afro. From a little six or seven year old, he stood as high as the trees. Apparently, he didn't have a car because we walked everywhere and we just stayed close in the area of my mom's apartment. I had the best seat in the neighborhood. I sat on his neck and shoulders as he walked me around and showed me off to everyone. I remember we stopped at the store and he bought me some Doritos, my favorite potato chips (hey if this book ever gets published I need to sign a contract with the Doritos company, lol). Then he took me home. That was our first official moment of bonding and establishing a relationship. I had a happy, good day. I believe I smiled the remaining of the day and probably a day or two after.

I recall two other occasions where my daddy came to pick me up to spend time. These visits and/or bonding moments happened within a short span of time after our very first visit. Second time, my mom tells me that my daddy is going to come pick me up as I was to sleep over to his house for the weekend. I was so excited! While I packed my clothes, all I kept thinking was "it's just going to be me and my daddy". I didn't know what to expect, but I just knew that every moment with him, I was his joy. That's how he made me feel. So of course, I waited with much anticipation for his arrival. By the time he came to get me, nightfall had arrived and again, we walked to our destination. As we proceeded to our destination, my daddy held me in his arms while holding my little "Going to Grandma's" suitcase. We finally make it to his home which didn't appear to be that far away. I remember he put me down and held my hand as we walked into the yard, then we walked up the steps to the porch; he then opened the screen door and began knocking on the front door as we stood there. I am so excited and I had the biggest smile on my face. Out of nowhere, the front door swings open hysterically and an old man (his father, my grandfather I assumed) appears holding and swinging a baseball bat in one hand and yelling at the top of his lungs "You get that child off my porch; I don't want that child in my house". I remember grabbing his hand so tight, pulling back and I was so scared. My daddy tried to reason with the old man for a few seconds and amongst the old man's yelling and screaming, but no luck. My daddy let go of the screen door and it slammed shut, he then picks me up, grabs my little "Going to Grandma's" suitcase and we quickly leave. I could tell my daddy was angry. He took me back home that night. On our way back to my house, all he kept telling me was to not be scared. When I arrived home, my mom was surprised to see us. All I did was ran straight to my room and cried. I couldn't understand why this old man who doesn't know me would not allow me to come to the house let alone let my daddy come in. A few moments later, my mother came to check on me to see if I was ok. I don't recall my mom asking me any questions, but I am pretty sure she asked my daddy. I felt sad and disappointed that I didn't get the chance to spend time with my father, but I was more frightened than anything.

The third time and final time we spent some time together was when he came to pick me one day and as we were walking (again walking) he tells me that he is taking me see my Aunts (his sisters) at their house. I was happy go-lucky to be with him. My skip had a beat. From what I recall, he was the only boy among his siblings. I believe a couple of his sisters shared a home together (I assume). We arrived to a small, grey house and as I walked inside, I remember spotting a hammock in one corner of the living room and there was so much sunlight coming through the windows. It was a hot and sunny day. Both of my Aunts were nice, happy to see me and so welcoming. It wasn't like the warm reception I received upon our last outing together. Of course, I was happy to be there. I was a bit nervous; yet smiling and making sure I didn't lose a step away from my father. One of the Aunts was obese (as a kid I would say she was fat) and the other aunt was regular-sized (please keep in mind I am remembering as a child and do not want to offend anyone). We spoke a few words as I looked around and that was that. We then left and I can't remember anything much more after that visit.

I also recall the time between the second and third visit with my daddy, I remember my younger siblings' father coming over to our apartment and he and my mother was arguing and I remember him having a problem with my daddy coming around. Thinking as an adult today, I can only assume my younger siblings' father and my mother must have still been seeing/dating each other and he didn't want my father coming around and interfering with what they had going on. I don't know, it's only an assumption.

Not that much time had passed and thus I believe we had moved again. I believe I had already turned (made the age of) seven. I remember it was the end of summer and school was about to start. So, one day I am playing in the room with my siblings and we are having a good ole' time. The curtains were wide open for the sunlight to seep through. My mother was a true believer of conserving electricity back then, as we (the kids) couldn't risk helping to make the light bill high. Playing with the curtains wide open was as if we were playing outside and we only had the room door cracked open a bit so our mom wouldn't hear so much noise and we then get in trouble yet just enough so she can still keep an ear out for us. Remember, we didn't like getting whippings. While we were playing, I believe my mother was in the kitchen cooking or something.

Well someone knocks at our door and of course we all try to peep to see who it is at the door coming into our home. We really didn't recognize this guy so we went about our business and kept on playing. Then our room door opened and the guy comes in. We all stopped playing and looked at him as if to say, "What you doing in our room?" And he said, "Mignon, let me talk to you". Looking at him reluctantly and confused as heck, with my siblings watching as well, I get up from playing and I walk to him as he guides me to the side of the bed. I sat at the top left side of the head of the bed (facing the foot of the bed). As I sat up against the headboard, he sort of knelt down on one knee in front of me. My siblings returned back to playing, though watching cautiously. In an ever so calm and low speaking tone, he says, "Hey, how are you doing?" I replied, "Fine". He says, "I want to ask you something". I said, "Ok". He says while softly touching my forehead, "Do you know where you get that forehead from?" I said, "My momma". He says, "No, you get that from me". I then said, "No, I get that from my momma". He says, "You know why you get that from me?" I didn't answer him; I just had a puzzled look on my face as to say, 'what are you talkin' about'. He then says, "You know why, 'cause I'm your father". My face gave the expression of saying, HUH!. Then I said (and only a child would say such a thing), "If you my daddy, then go buy me a Trapper Keeper?" He says, "Do you need this Trapper Keeper?" And I said, "Yes, I need it for school". He says, "Is that what you want my baby?" I replied, "Yes". He then says, "I'm telling you, I am your father." I say, "Ok". He then gets up and leaves the room. I go back to playing and my siblings ask me what he wanted and I told them that he said he my daddy. So, later on that day, the man who said and claimed to be my daddy comes back with the Trapper Keeper. Of course, I was shocked and all I remember saying to myself, "He must be my daddy" but 'what about my other daddy". While he's handing me the bag with the Trapper Keeper inside, he says, "Here you go my baby". Later on my momma asks me what he said and I told her that he said he was my daddy. My momma tells me, "don't you believe what he said; you already know who your daddy is". And I said, "But...." And she cuts me off saying, "You heard what I told you?" I am like, "yes ma'am" and I leave and go play with my new Trapper Keeper.

Just to let you know, the man stated above apparently was not a stranger to the home as he was my mom's brother-in-law. One of my mom's sisters had married his brother. So my mom knew him because he was, I guess, part of the family.

Again, time has passed by and I am now about thirteen years old. At this time, my mom was dating my stepdad in which they had been dating since my age of nine. During the summertime of me turning thirteen, I noticed one day that all my siblings had gone to be with their other extended families and I was home alone. Meaning, I had no one to play with, no siblings to talk to, and there weren't any girls my age to hang around with in the neighborhood. On this particular day, it dawned on me (cause I was literally the only child home at the time) that over the years all my siblings would leave on weekends and sometimes during summers to go spend time with their fathers and their other extended families and I would be left alone at home.

Now you may ask, well, what were you doing all this time for you not to notice any time sooner? During those times, I would either have a sleepover at either one of my mom's sister houses or I would babysit children (family and friends of family) and earn a little money, hang out with a friend from school or be busy with extracurricular activities with school. So, I would somewhat be occupied. From time-to-time (not too often), I would sometimes wonder 'why my dad wasn't around and if I had done anything for him to not be around'. At some point, it became too much to think about and I guess I just didn't really bother going to my mother about it.

I was always going over to visit one of my aunt and uncle (my mom's sister and brother-in-law) and my

37

cousin(s). This particular family, I would sleep over all the time. I had so much fun with them. I so loved being around them and with my cousins. You know, that family introduced me to my first pair of pantyhose for girls my age. I knew they were made for adults but never thought they made pantyhose in young girl sizes. They studied a different religion from me but that never mattered, I would attend and learn their way of church. Like I said, that never mattered, I just wanted to hang out with my cousins and be with family.

My other aunt, she was of the same religion and she and my uncle had a daughter and I was like the big sister and the big helper when I would visit them. They are a fun couple and I would say they are both some comedians; all the adults enjoyed hanging out at their house all the time. They always had family events to attend and I was right along with them. They took me in and made me feel special as if I was their daughter and it was just so quiet and peaceful within their home. Don't get me wrong, I love my brothers and sister, but a little me time was always a good time. So at times, I would get a chance of being spoiled.

But anyway, on this particular day, I told my mother that it wasn't fair and that I wanted to go to my daddy's house. I asked here, "Where's my daddy?" She never answered me. So, I kept asking and yet she never answered me. She knew what I was asking and she clearly heard my question, but she just didn't give a reply. I couldn't understand why she was ignoring me, why she was not responding to me and that became troubling to me. While standing in the kitchen area, my stepdad says, "I think you better tell her".

And I said, "Tell me what?" And I repeated that statement a couple more times, "Tell me what?", "Tell me what?" Hey, I wasn't trying to get a whipping in the process so I had to watch myself. My mom kept pacing the floor from the bedroom through the kitchen to the living room and not saying anything. I watched her do this several times. Then my stepdad tells me to have a seat at the kitchen table. I respond to him saying, "Tell me what?" My stepdad then proceeds to tell me that my father (who my mom says is my father) had died when I was about the age of seven. I am like died, how? My eyes began tearing up. He says, "In a house fire." So, I am sitting there at the table and my heart is terribly broken, I feel lost and my eyes are filled with tears while my mom is still pacing back and forth from room to room as if to pretend she doesn't hear our discussion. My mind and my thoughts were racing inside my head, racing inside my head, racing inside my head as I tried to gather up time frames and put together the years of gaps. I was shocked, confused and numb all at the same time.

As I thought to myself and said aloud, "So this whole time I thought he didn't want to be in my life and he can't because he's dead?" By this time, I am boo-hoo crying. At that moment I realized that for all those years my father was not around, I had been harboring a little anger towards him in the fact that he just stopped visiting me. I felt so much guilt for being a bit angry and I guess that's why I immediately burst out in tears. My stepfather then proceeds to tell me the story of how my father died. He says, well, he heard that my father was on some medication and just before he went to sleep he had decided to smoke a cigarette and in the process of smoking the cigarette, he fell asleep. Apparently, the medication heavily sedated him. The sheets caught fire thus burning him, the bed, and the house. Now, mind you, my mother is still pacing the floor back and forth from room to room as if to pretend she doesn't hear our discussion. Then all the questions came pouring out. "Well, why my momma never told me this when it happened?" and "Did she attend the funeral?" "Why didn't she take me to the funeral?" "Where is he buried?" "Where is his grave?" "Did anybody attend the funeral on my behalf?" My stepdad said, "Yes, I attended the funeral for you." I sincerely thanked him from the bottom of my heart. Now, he could have just been saying that to pick my spirits up or he could have been telling the truth. But knowing who and how his character was, I believed he told me the truth at that time. I mean, my own mother wasn't trying to tell me anything.

But listen to this. It didn't dawn to me (present time now) until I was eating lunch with my girlfriend that I thought, hold up, how was he able to attend the funeral when he came into my life when I was nine years old when he stated that my dad was killed at the age of seven. So was my stepdad telling me this just to shut me up or calm me down or was he indeed dating my mother for a few years before she introduced him to us (the children)? What were his reason(s)? What compelled him to feel the need to step in for my mother? I don't know. I wonder from whom or where he received his information about my father. Was it my mother that told him of such story, or was it from rumors of the streets, or was it from my mother's family members? If he didn't really attend the funeral, he was quick on his feet back then because stating his attendance calmed me down and I was ok that someone had at least represented me. I will have to ask him about this, FOR SURE!!!!!

Ok, where was I? Now, the whole time my stepdad is telling me this, my mother not at all once came to neither confirm nor deny what he said, yet she continued to pace back and forth from room to room listening. I then ask my stepdad, "What funeral home buried him and what cemetery was his grave?" My stepdad stated he could not remember. I believe my stepdad was hurt for me, he felt my pain, my sorrow and I think right then at that moment he unconditionally, unconsciously decided that he was going to just always be there for me (I can't explain it, it's just how the unspoken emotions within our conversation went about). I said, to myself and aloud, "Ok" while trying to wipe my tears and toughen up a bit. Within my own deep thoughts, I realized I went from being upset with my father to being upset with myself that I had the thought of my father not wanting to be around me, and to think, there was a more valid reason as to why he couldn't. I wasn't at all happy that my father had passed yet I felt vindicated that he just didn't desert me and left me all alone. At that time, I believe I had made peace within myself and released those negative emotions I once felt.

In counseling myself, I guess I validated him and his non-presence by placing the guilt (of my negative thoughts about him) on myself. It's like, I cleared his name, his actions (non-actions really). To validate me and make right of the negative thoughts I once had, I decided to search every funeral home located in my hometown until I found his death certificate. I literally called almost every funeral home and asked if they had buried my father. The only information the funeral home administrative office needed was a name to check/verify their records. I hadn't told anyone that I was doing this, not even my mother. This was done on my own accord. Well after searching and calling, I eventually found the funeral home and they were non-hesitant, willing to give me a copy of my father's death certificate. Because of the support my stepdad had given me previously, I asked him if he would take me over to the funeral home to pick it up, he agreed and he did. I was the happiest child in the world because I had a piece of my father to hold on to and I knew where I belonged. I kept his death certificate close to me and carried it around in my purse for years, into my adult life. That death certificate (piece of paper) validated that I have a place of belonging and from hence I came.

Now, as I am growing up it is brought to my attention that I am attending middle and high school with my cousins from my "biological" dad side (the one that passed away). It is at this time, my mom began telling me more of my father's family. The funny thing is she would see that side of the family from time to time because we all lived in the same city. According to what my mom says, some of my father's family members spoke to her (speaking terms) and some didn't. Now my mom is telling me who I am kin to and where aunts and kin folk live (reside). I am not exactly sure of timeframe, but I remember her telling me I had an older half-brother. I was told his name, where he lived and what he did for a living. No doubt, I was happy because a part of my dad was still out there that I had not yet met and yet we were blood related. I was curious to know and wanted to see if he (half-brother) was tall like our father as well as looked like him. Based upon the age of when I met our father, I only had what I like to call, a "childhood glimpse" of him so to see if this half-brother had a resemblance would have been nice. Well, there was no way of me finding that out any time soon. From time to time, the cousins I knew of and spoke to would always tell me after the fact that my half-brother was in town. The chance of ever meeting him any time soon always seemed unlikely. Therefore, like any other person, I went on with life as I knew it.

We thus moved again, and now, I go about my life feeling ok, but I knew that parts of my life just weren't complete. I begin a quest to somehow find out who my paternal grandmother is. I definitely was not thinking or trying to locate my paternal grandfather, the way he treated (frightened) me back in the day when I was younger, chèr please. I asked my mom to tell me anything that she could possibly remember as well as see if she can somehow find out more information if she by chance runs into one of my aunts again. She told me what she could remember and she also tells me that she believes that my paternal grandmother may be living around the corner from us. My mouth dropped and I'm like, 'HUH'. So, I am now asking her if she could remember the house number or even the color of the house. She tells me the color of the house and I am so happy inside cause this would be another gap I can finally close. Personally, I think my mother knew all along but didn't want to deal with it until I asked, I really don't think she thought I was even going to ask. But anyway, I received the information I needed to proceed on my quest. It was as if I was on a purposeful mission, but not necessarily a deliberate mission. If the cards dealt to me appeared to give me an opportunity and if my mind was aligned with the opportunity (such as a thought, which may have prompt a question, which may have prompt some digging, i.e. investigation), I think God just placed me in a position with some confidence to take subtle action.

Every day, for about a week, I walk the neighborhood trying to determine which houses have the color my mom referenced and trying to wean out those that don't quite measure up. I stumbled upon one particular house that seems to match to a tee. And, every day I struggled with finding enough confidence and courage within me to simply walk up to the door and knock. I recognized that I had been there before because I remember walking the neighborhood when I was younger, selling Girl Scouts cookies when I was just a Brownie Scout. We moved a lot and sometimes the houses we moved to would be within the same vicinity of the last location (close by). Unfortunately, it takes me a couple of weeks to muster up some confidence, but I finally get the nerve to make a move.

This one particular day, I told myself, I said "self, what do you have to lose, either they accept you or they don't, so what's it going to be". I remember that day clearly. I told my mother I would be right back that I was going for a walk in the neighborhood. She said 'ok', and for me to 'stay in this neighborhood'. I thought to myself, Oh sure, I will be just around the corner. She didn't know I was going, I don't think... Well, it felt like it took me forever to get to her house and it was literally around the corner. It was as if the street was stretching farther and farther away as I was walking. Like one street over from our house. The entire walk, I was mentally pumping myself up with confidence that I could actually do this. I knew my mother wasn't going to come with me and she would have probably forbade me from going, according to the way she said her relationship was with them from the beginning and the fact that she stated she didn't want to have anything to do with them. So, I was definitely on my own if I wanted to do this. I don't even believe my siblings were even home at the time, they usually would sometimes go to their father's during the weekend. Yes, I was STILL the only child remaining at home for weekends.

I manage to get there and as I walked to the front door, I took a big deep breath and knocked with my hardest knock. And all of a sudden an older lady comes to the door. I say "hello" and she asks if she can help me. I proceed to ask if she was who I thought she was and she says yes. I then say, "yes ma'am, well, I am" and I state my name and I tell her that I am her son's daughter and ask if she knows about me. She froze for a second holding on to the frame of the front door and my heart dropped because I didn't know what to think or what to do next. We were both literally stood there at a pause as if in immediate shock. As I stood there, she somehow comes through and she asks if I wanted to come in and I agreed. I followed her to the living room and she says for me to have a seat on the couch. I walked in looking around to see what was what and to see if anyone else was there. As I sat down, I noticed she had an 11x17 photo, maybe larger, of my dad on the wall. I sat up and walked over to the picture to get an even closer look and told her yes that is how I remember he looked. Big tears came to my eyes and I proceeded to ask her if she had any other pictures she could possibly give to me so I could have one. She flat out, quickly and not-so-pleasantly told me "No", that that was the only picture she had of her son and that all the rest of the pictures burned in the fire. In my mind, I quickly thought to myself, 'you only have one picture, really, just the one'. My spirit couldn't accept that and the negativity I was receiving from her didn't sit too well with me either, but what was I to do. I couldn't tell her she was lying to me, although I surely thought it. Thus, I just accepted it and sat there in her house just looking around. There wasn't much of a conversation. She didn't ask about my mother or any other family members. She did ask how I was doing and what grade I was in. It was as if she was not at all interested in me, my thoughts, my life, nothing. That was pretty much it, so I told her that I didn't want to keep her and I at least wanted to meet and see her. She proceeded with an ok and I left.

Now during my walk home, I contemplated over all the things that had just occurred. First thing that came to mind was when she said 'No' about the pictures, I remember feeling like she was disgusted by me, really didn't care for me being there and I could definitely sense that she really didn't want to have a relationship with me. Next, I thought back to what my mother had previously told me about them and it made more sense, maybe they are the way they are but it was confusing as to why she would be like that with me. I didn't do nor have I done anything to her. What was it? What could it be? I couldn't figure it out and once again, I just had to accept it and move on.

To answer your thought, yes, yes. I told my mother about my visit when I returned home. Mind you, I did not inform her while being within the same room with her. I calmly yelled it out to her from another room. Conversation started out with, "hey momma, I went to visit my grandmother around the corner today". She replied or should I say yelled, "You did what!" Based upon her tone, I don't think she was pretty happy with me. She placed a strong stern emphasis on the word 'what'. Trust me. I believe she may have paused and thought for a quick second, 'wait I need more information' because her demeanor somehow shifted to a more subtle approach. Besides, I knew she wanted to know more about the visit and not have me shut down keeping my responses simple. When I told her what happened, she really didn't say much during nor afterwards. I thought she may have been thinking that what she told me previously was confirmation for her as it should be for me (like an 'I told you so' type of thing).

Fast forward.

At this time, I am a young adult living on my own about the age of 20 turning 21 that summer. The time of year was around the Fourth of July weekend. During this time in my life, I lived in a pretty decent duplex/townhouse and the complex was located off of a frontage road which was parallel to the highway/thruway. While hanging outside within my apartment complex with some friends that stopped by to make a quick visit, a red Toyota 4Runner kept passing back and forth on the thruway. That vehicle had made so many trips to where we all noticed and commented about it. Shoot, it was as if he/she was lost and it was pretty hard not to notice a red vehicle constantly passing by. Well, we continued on with our visit, making plans to have fun for the weekend.

So, later that day, my girlfriend and I decided to go take a ride around the city to see where the happening spots were, more like a joyride before we partook in our evening plans. Then, out of nowhere, I noticed the Red Toyota 4Runner is on the same two-lane road driving toward us on the opposite lane. We both noticed it was a guy driving. Traffic is moving at an all-time slow pace as if it was a car show or something. It was somewhat like a daytime party scene. So, I asked my girlfriend whom was driving (remember, I am a walker—I got it from my father, so I had no car) to drive real slow when we approach the red vehicle 'cause I wanted to just get a glimpse of who was driving the Red Toyota 4Runner. I told her that that was the same vehicle that kept driving back and forth on the thruway by my apartment and I was just curious to see who it was that kept making the same trip as if they were lost. Trust me, it was that many trips. Well, she did and decides to make contact with the driver and told him to meet us a rally point nearby. Yes, she was that bold. He agreed and met us at the rally point she requested.

While my girlfriend was making that love connection with him, he was sort of admiring my haircut/hairstyle and states that he is a barber. Then, he gives us his business card. During his chit chat with my girlfriend and admiring, he had written on the back of the card the number to the place/location where he would be staying while in town. As I am reading the card, silently I say to myself—"WHAT!" You won't believe it, but it had the same name of the half-brother I was searching for, the same profession and the same location of state residence based upon what I was told by family members. Immediately, something within me automatically knew, this dude is my half-brother. And I couldn't say anything to my girlfriend because I wasn't exactly sure and I didn't want to rain on her parade of making that love connection. So, I remained at awe and left it at that.

The evening came and went. It was about eleven p.m. when I arrived at home and mentally I kept telling myself, 'girl you need to call him'. I assure you, I knew in my bones that he was the half-brother I was so eagerly searching for. I was so excited; as I sat on the edge of my bed, I would rock back and forth in excitement knowing that another puzzle piece is finally being put together. But, I was oh so nervous and a bit afraid. One, I needed to find the push to go and make that phone call. Two, how was I going to convince a stranger that I was his half-sister and we in fact had the same father without him thinking I was creepy and weird.

What words do I say, how do I begin the conversation, what if he hangs up on me, what if he doesn't believe me, what if he isn't who I think he is, do I want to embarrass myself, is it that serious enough for me to find out? The mental battle and struggle was not an easy one. I fought with myself for about two hours and then I finally convinced myself that I could do it. I had gotten out of bed and sat on the floor on my knees. I don't know why, I felt more comfortable there. I first, retrieved my father's death certificate from my purse (where it had been for years) and I placed it next to the business card on the floor. I looked at both and I told myself, this has to be him because everything I was told about him matches up perfectly. Nervous out of my mind, I first called the number he had given, and by the way, it is now one a.m. in the morning. On the other end of the phone call, a little old lady answered and she stated he was not there, that he had already left to go back to his home and she gave me the timeframe of when he left. I immediately apologized for calling her home that early in the morning and told her that I had no idea of the residence the number was related to. She understood and we hung up. At this time, I began to determine what time he may arrive home or in the city at least given the fact that he was traveling from out of town and all. I sort of had an idea of when he was to return.

Question is, what should I do? Do I wait until the next day, or wait a few more hours then call or should I call and leave a message for him to call me back. Mental struggle again. I chose to do the last option. Ok, I had to get a game plan of what exactly I was going to say. I hoped there was an answering machine to leave a message yet if one wasn't available, I would just call back. Safe enough.

I am dialing the numbers and the phone proceeds to ring, and guess what, he answers the phone. I was shocked because I thought he would be there later, but his grandmother didn't know he had left earlier than what she stated according to what he said. Anyway, I asked him if he remembered me and stated yes. So then, as nervous as I was, I tell him that I had to ask him a few questions and that the questions may sound weird but that I needed him to answer. Without hesitation, he agreed (I am pretty sure he was expecting me to ask questions in reference of getting to know him, little did he know). First question: I asked if his father's name and birth date was blank and blank, and he replied yes. He thought it was a bit weird but not too unusual as he stated. Second question: I asked if his father was killed in a house fire, and he replied yes. Then he added in a confused and puzzled tone, 'how do you know this?' I know at this time I now have his full attention, though I don't know for how long, so I just continue to ask questions back to back. Third question: I asked if his grandmother was blank and blank, and he replied yes. Last few questions asked inquired whether he knew of a few other people and he replied yes to each one. I boldly but calmly, flat out told him, I believe you are my half-brother. Although I was not there to see with mine own eyes, I could immediately tell he was in a state of shock. There was a silent pause because I didn't know what to say next and I wasn't sure if he had hung up the phone on me. Think about it, 1) it was real early in the morning (almost three a.m.) and 2) to hear some mess like this. I proceed with a 'Hello' and he says "are you serious?" I told him that I was not playing around and that I had the death certificate of our father sitting right in front of me. As proof, I began to read it to him to justify my allegation.

I could tell he was still in shock. I too wasn't really sure if this was really happening, although I was really excited inside. I told him that it has been several years that I knew of him. I confirmed a few other things for him to the point where we are both actually convincing each other that this is so. All of a sudden the mood of the conversation shifts. I then sense that he is somewhat upset at this point. His next comment was that he has to call his mother and I interrupted saying "at this time in the morning" and he is like, "yes, at this time". I suggested he didn't awake her and to just wait a few more hours until daybreak. He stated he needed to find out right then and there if his mother knew of what I was saying as well as if this were to be of some truth. Before we hung up, he assured me that he would call me right back. I understood his ploy to verify; me personally, I wasn't going to give up information about myself not knowing who in the world I was talking to. Our conversation ended and I assumed he called his mother, yes, at three a.m. in the morning.

As I sat on my knees and I just leaned forward and took a deep breath. I remember thinking to myself, "I can't believe this is happening. Did this just really happen?" I kept repeating to myself, "I can't believe I found my brother. Is it really him?" I just sat there in amazement and excitement and a bit worrisome because I wasn't sure if his mother knew anything about me or the situation of his father. So, I just sat there waiting and waiting and waiting for him to call back. While I sat there, I recalled to myself all the events of how everything happened for us to be at this point. I thought, "this had to be God's plan being that we somehow out-of-the-clear-blue-sky meet in such a way". I wait, and I wait. And I wait, and I wait, anxiously.

A few hours had passed because I am noticing the sun is beginning to rise. Then my phone rings and just about scares the 'bajeebas' out of me. Nervously, I answer with a hint of timidness in my voice and my half-brother is on the line and I could tell he had been crying, so, I ask him if he was ok. He replies, "Yes" and then he says, "I have my mom on the line too". I just sat there because I didn't know what to say to her. She calls my name and states she wants to apologize to me. Again, I didn't know what to say exactly although I did accept her apology. She begins to cry and my brother is crying, now we all crying, boo-hoo crying. He hangs up with his mom and we remain on the phone to talk more. From what I gathered, we were the only two children of our father.

Although our conversation wasn't very long, we manage to get a few of the important things out of the way. I know we were both in awe with confusion and with excitement wrapped around it. He begins to tell me that his mom stated it was true that he has a half-sister, and that he didn't know about me at all, how he was a tad bit upset with his mother for not saying anything about it, and how he lost out on growing up with me, and how he didn't have anything but a picture of our dad. I told him that I was still in shock of how all of this happened and that I couldn't believe it. I guess we were at the right place, at the right time because I sure didn't have a current or any type of plan to search for him.

Somehow I had a hunch after reading his business card and I just had to take a chance at calling 'cause I needed to know and I needed to close some of the gaps within my life. Conversation continues and he tells me about his baby sisters, his mom and stepdad and about the cousins we have that I haven't met yet, about his career and where he works. I tell him about his two nieces he had and try to pan out the story of how I came about between my mom and our dad (only went by the info my mother told me). In some way, I felt that we were both trying to determine how each other felt without really asking or saying so. I grew up knowing I had a half-brother, so it wasn't as difficult for me to take in the shock but on the other hand, he had no clue, no idea of a half-sister, so I could empathize with what he may have been feeling. We promised to keep in touch and our phone call then ended. Just know a few weeks later, I was turning 21 and as a birthday present to myself I manage to plan a trip to visit him and his family.

Well the next summer, now I am about the age of twenty-two, I decided to take a vacation trip to see my aunt, uncle and cousins in which over the years they had moved to another state. My kids and I go and we had a blast. Every so often, my uncle would always make a comment in reference to me being related (kinship) to him twice. He would always make it seem as a joke of some sort. I would always wonder why does he continue repeating/saying the same thing to me. Of course we were related; he married my mother's sister. I just thought he flew over the coo coo's nest instead of landing in it. Well, it went over my head.

Moving on.

Years and time has passed and I believe I am a full-grown adult (so I like to say). I am about the age of thirty-three, soon to be thirty-four and I am married, have two more children, have experienced a few things, traveled a few places and lived in a few states while accomplishing plenty (Thanks *be* to the LORD). The same aunt and uncle, I have previously spoke about, invites me and my family to join them in celebrating the college graduation of their youngest child. This was to occur during the summertime right before my birthday. My family and I decided to attend the graduation which wasn't that far from where we currently lived. I am all excited because it had been a few years since I had seen my relatives. These are the same family members I grew up with and had so much fun. Can't tell a fib, they were a fun bunch.

Anyways, we arrived a few minutes after the ceremony began. Unfortunately, we weren't able to sit with all the family because we arrived at a later time (driving from a different city and all). All in all, we enjoyed the graduation. At this time, the graduation ceremony is over. It was different from what I had normally experienced at a college graduation. Everyone had been released to meet the graduates outside of the auditorium and at the same time we (my family and I) were also going to meet and gather with the rest of the family so we can meet the new graduate altogether. Well, as soon as my family and I arrive outside, I began searching for my relatives. From this point of the graduation event, everything began to happen very quickly as if standing in a spinning room and you can't stop it from spinning.

As soon as my immediate family was able to meet up together with the others, out of nowhere my aunt says to me aloud, 'your dad is here'. My face scrunched up and had the most puzzling expression on it and my husband's eyes darted at me as I turned and looked at him. So this guy walks up to me and says "hey my daughter, how you been doing". My facial and verbal expression is like, 'what the f@#$'. My aunt proceeds with telling his children, 'hey kids, this is your big sister; y'all take a picture'. Then, bim bam boom, cameras come from out of the woodworks like paparazzi and everyone is quickly gathering around us for pictures. Aloud, my aunt says to my children as well as his children 'look kids these are your aunts and uncles and these are your nieces and nephews; y'all related'. Mind you all the kids are almost or just about the same ages. My husband and children are staring at me, shocked and clueless as to say what in the heck is going on and I am still in the 'WTF' state of mind while we all are being shoved around to take photos. All you could hear was "Y'all get like this, move over here, move over there, you take a knee, smile, tilt your head up, take off your shades, everybody look this way, SAY CHEESE!" That happened at least four to five times, back-to-back.

Seemed like a lifetime of chaos. Again, my husband is looking at me and I mumbled under my breath so sternly, "GO GET THE CAR!" My husband with an ever so kind smile hastily gathered our children and took them to the car with him while I stayed and waited for him to come pick me up so things didn't appear as if we were anxious to leave.

While standing there, I was then told that the graduation dinner was being held at a particular restaurant in which the graduate and her parents enjoyed dining. Next, I was asked to attend. Then I was told that I must attend. I simply stated that I needed to check with my husband and would call them via cell phone from the car to let them know if we would attend or decide to get on the road and travel back home. They kept insisting we follow them to the restaurant. My husband pulls up in the car and of course without wasting any more time, I hopped on in. I proceed to tell my husband of their insistence of us following them to the restaurant and my aunt and uncle wouldn't take 'NO' for an answer. Being shocked and all, I honestly didn't want to be mean because this is the family I always had fun with and thought well maybe since we going to a restaurant (a public area) it won't be so bad. My husband and I just told them that we would meet them there.

You see, taking pictures did not affect me at all; it was the ambush of telling me that this guy is my father and that the whole family knew all along, that my kids were his grandchildren, that his kids were my kids' aunts and uncles, and how my kids were their kids' nieces and nephews. Darn, that was a mouthful. And at this point, I am totally distraught.

Remember earlier in the story, I told you about a man that came over to my house and sat me down and asked where I received my forehead? Well, it appears this is the same guy which is my uncle's brother that they (aunt and uncle) as well as he (mystery dad) are claiming to be my father. Clearly, the story doesn't end here.

Well, during the ride to the restaurant, my husband and kids are asking me question after question that I really didn't have an answer for. Not to mention, they were making fun of me in the process. They were saying, "You better be good or we're going to tell your daddy" or "don't yell at us, or we're going to tell your daddy". They kept going on and on. They made the situation funny for me to get a laugh during the time of my confusion and chaos.

With all this confusion and chaos going on and while we were on the way to the restaurant, I decided to contact my mother because she would know the truth and I really wanted to know if it was possible, at all, that he could be my biological father. I also wanted her to confirm it wasn't so I could defend her honor and squash all the 'he say, she say' bit. I dialed her number, she picks up and I proceed to explain what was going on and what had happened a few moments prior to me calling her. Next, I ask, "ok mother, can you, at all, remember and tell me if you and he slept together at least one time?" I believe I asked her that question at least three times. She said 'NO' the first two times and on the third time, my cell phone was screaming at me. She was so loud and in surround sound that I held the cell phone up in the air and my husband and kids heard her. She cussed me out to the third degree. She said, "I already told you who your f'ing daddy is", "don't be questioning me and questioning what I f'ing say", and last, "I did not f'ing sleep with him, not at all, not even one time". I didn't take any offense to anything she stated or the cussing. I was cool about it, but my husband and our children were shocked at the words she used. My focus was not the cuss words but more on the answers she gave. I told her that I just wanted to know so I could defend her and her word against anyone if anything 'pops off' at the restaurant.

My husband and kids clowned (made fun) me about the "Daddy" situation the entire ride to the restaurant.

In my mom's and I defense, I was prepared for whatever was to occur at the restaurant.

We arrived to the restaurant and it appears there were no reservations made prior to attending and it was quite a bit of people that showed up to eat and celebrate with the graduate and her family. So it took a while to be seated and we didn't get to sit amongst each other. We were seated in different areas of the restaurant. The restaurant patrons tried to do the best they could, given there were no reservations. I believe we had three different tables and they were all segregated and separated to some extent from each other. To be nice and cordial, I walked to my aunt and uncle's table to speak to them and as soon as I arrive, she says to the assumed father's kids, "this is y'all big sister". I immediately stopped her and nicely corrected her by stating, "Auntie don't say that to those kids, you don't know if that is true and I sure don't want them to go through what I went through, so don't say that". She was a bit shocked and I guess she understood because I didn't sense any tension from her. So, we continued to speak a bit and I went back to my table.

At this point, I was ready to leave and really didn't have much of an appetite.

Moments later, as we decide we are leaving it appears everyone is just about ready to head out and we all get up and proceed outside to the front of the restaurant to say our goodbyes and all. Of course, my aunt and uncle just couldn't leave well alone. Here they go again bringing up the talk that this guy is my father. This guy is talking to me and asking about how we can keep in touch (and sh't like that). I am like 'keep in touch with whom'? My husband was looking towards me and became a bit annoyed as if to say 'why are they bum-rushing his wife'. Then, my husband approaches the guy (who claim is my father) and they go off to the side to talk somewhat privately (y'all thought I was going to say to fight).

My aunt and uncle pours out every possible circumstance or story they could remember to keep my attention focused on them and the assumed truth that their brother is my dad, that the entire family (maternal and paternal sides) knew and just never said anything, that my maternal grandmother knew and she took that information to her grave (May She Rest In Peace), that my mom kept him (this guy) from me, how my mom had three heart attacks and told the family to not to say anything to any of her children because she didn't want her children to know, how I resembled their (paternal) side of the family more, explaining how it all happened between my mom and their brother, the timeframe I was conceived (my inner thought was like were y'all there), how their brother used to give my mom money as child support and how they (mom and dad) were the best of friends that used to hang out all the time. They (aunt and uncle) went back and forth between the two of them, not coming up for air confirming and seconding the motion of each other's words. Just imagine, I was standing there looking to and fro like a pendulum at my aunt and uncle as each told their story at the same time.

This was too much for me and I was fed up beyond the point of pisstivity (if that's a word). I just sat down in the rocking chair located in front of the restaurant and cried. From a distance, my husband turned around and seen me sitting there with my head down, crying and he rushes over and said, "Let's go, we are leaving." My aunt was like trying to console me, but damage was done. The guy was still persistent in trying to find a way to stay in touch. He made it very evident and clear, standing his ground and his word that he was my biological father. I made it very clear to him that I had spoken with my mother and she stated otherwise. Next, my husband held me in his arms and told me not to cry as we proceed to leave.

Well, at this point the guy insists on giving us his contact information and I didn't refuse from taking it. I felt if I ever had any questions, I would be able to contact him for answers. We eventually leave the restaurant and make our journey back to our home. During the ride home, my husband couldn't help but think aloud why this man was so deliberate at making this a big deal even to the point of having help in broadcasting it to me, because my aunt and uncle didn't miss a beat. Well, my husband proceeds to tell me of the conversation he and the guy had while at the restaurant. My husband stated that the guy was very hesitant and worrisome to even bring it up simply because he was not sure how I would respond being that I am an adult now nor did he not know how my husband would react as well. Although, he felt it was so important that he needed to say something.

Now I have so many questions running through my mind and I am trying to put some pieces of the puzzle (answers) together. I basically was conversing to myself, within myself, but aloud, so my husband knew what was on my mind. I immediately thought, 'would my momma lie to me? No, she wouldn't lie to me'. I just called her earlier and she clearly said 'NO' with a few cuss words attached. But, why would he (the guy), my aunt and uncle make it such a big deal, really? Could it possibly be as such? Uh-uh. No way, no how. I know who my daddy is and there is no way that all these years---uh-uh. Man, get out of here. I also thought, my mother would not have gotten that defensive if she wasn't so sure of herself. My husband stated, she could have been defensive just to throw you off (don't quote me on the exact wording but in that sense). Who knows? In the end, I sided with my mother. I felt she would know and she knew.

As I stated previously, this incident happened during the summertime. Since that confrontation, only a few months passed and that ordeal had been weighing very heavy on my mind. I mean real heavy. Every once and a while, my husband would bring it up again and I would ever so politely brush it off trying to avoid it all. I came to a point where I just couldn't stand it anymore. I had a plan and I didn't tell my husband or anyone of the matter, what I was preparing to do until I knew exactly what I was up against. My plan was to go online and search for DNA places near his (the guy) local residence or in the surrounding area of his hometown. Low and behold, there is a company listed and its location is close by. So, I called the company for any and all information. Again, neither my husband nor anyone had a clue of what was going on. I explained to the representative of the company my situation and asked her to help me determine the best solution. I received all the information I could possibly gather: products, validity, prices, location and times of operation. The representative insisted and eagerly agreed to grant me an appointment on a weekend day just to make this happen because all too often children end up not knowing who their father is and the child(ren) suffers in the end as well as the fact that I was traveling from such a far distance. I scheduled and confirmed the appointment. Officially finding out if this guy is my father has to happen and there be no turning back. Now that the appointment is scheduled and confirmed, I informed my husband and without a shadow of any doubt, he is very SUPPORTIVE. My next mission was to call this guy to see how serious he was about claiming to be my father.

I decided to call him (the guy) the next morning while at work during my morning break and I told him of my plans to find out if he really is my father. I told him I would pay for everything and provided him with the location and appointment information and he confirmed he would show up for the appointment. This was the first conversation we had. Now, all I do is wait until the appointment date and time. Part one of what I call the 'nerve wrecking' experience. At this point, the only other persons besides me who knew of my plans were my husband, this guy and the guy's wife (I assume).

Days, weeks passed and it is time to travel to attend the appointment. We make our travels there the night before the appointment date and decided to stay with one of my siblings. Now mind you, I hadn't even told my sibling with whom we were staying with about the matter. The next day, my husband and I get up real early around 6:30 a.m. to ensure we didn't miss the appointment. We arrived early and we waited until he (the guy) arrives. I told my husband, I didn't care if I had to drive pick him up from his house; he was going to get to this appointment. Oh, it's going to happen, I was definitely determined. Well to my surprise, he shows up. Next, we completed all the necessary paperwork and make full payment. Do you know he paid for half of the test, yes, he paid half. I was totally surprised. In my opinion, he was making this accusation of his to be so believable. Who would actually go through all of this and believe they are not the father. Well, some men do go through it to prove they are not the father, so this goes hand-in-hand. Then, we proceed with taking a DNA test. Part two of the nerve wrecking experience. Once we finished, we spoke briefly for a few minutes or so and my husband and I leave. During the DNA test, we were told that the test results process would take about a week or so and that we would receive a phone call and an email of the results.

So we wait. Part three of the nerve wrecking experience.

A few weeks have passed and my husband and I are traveling to his hometown this particular weekend due to attending a dinner in honor of one of his best friends whom was fighting the battle of a serious ailment. We weren't exactly sure as to what specific date the DNA test results would be provided, but we were anticipating the results any day now. During our trip, my concern and focus was on my husband grieving the notion of his best friend's ailment and of him possibly losing his best friend soon. Our travels consisted of passing through my hometown to get to his hometown where the dinner was to take place. As we are cruising along and are about to approach the exit which we take to go to my hometown; I received a phone call from an unknown number. So, I answered the phone and to my surprise, it is the representative from the DNA office ready to provide me with the results. I personally was not prepared mentally at that time, because I was so focused on ensuring my husband was ok during his time of need, yet I was not about to have them call me back at another time with the results. I wanted to know and I believe my husband wanted to know as well.

In a way, I think my husband and I needed something else to think about and this was the perfect drama to shift our thoughts just for a moment. I provided all the required information in order for me to receive the DNA test results via a phone call. While I held my breath, I heard blah, blah, blah, blah.......blah, blah, blah......99.9999%.......blah, blah, blah, BLAH! The "blah, blah" represented the medical language/terminology in which the representative was required to read to me. I replied with, "Can you please repeat that in ENGLISH"? The representative replied, 99.9999% he is your biological father. I damn near choked on hearing those words! While I was shocked, surprised, confused, almost without words (speechless), I replied, "are you serious!?" and the representative confirmed once more. With nothing else to say or do, I was able to say thank you and request that the DNA test results be sent via my email address as well as mailed, originals, no copies. The DNA representative agreed and our phone call ended.

So, my husband is just staring at me, with the facial expression of WHAT DID THEY SAY. I said to him, "I was just told that this guy is my real daddy". All my husband could say is 'whaaaatttt'. By the time I hung up the phone, we were passing up the exit to my hometown and my husband asks "do you want to stop now and talk to your mother about this?" I thought about it for a quick second and I replied "No, and that I will need more time to deal with her and besides we were on another mission." So, I told him I could wait until Sunday when we are on our way back home. I could tell my husband was very concerned about me, I guess it was the empty, blank and f'd up look I had upon my face. I felt as so and I knew he saw it.

Neither one of us said a single word for a few minutes. I didn't hear so much silence before, even the noise outside the vehicle and the white noise within the car didn't exist to me. Pure silence. I don't believe either one of us knew exactly what to say about the news we just heard. My husband may have thought that if he would have said something I might have snapped. I want to say that, for a second, I believe I stepped outside of my body and watched myself from the backseat and I just sat there, no expression whatsoever. I knew, even though we didn't say, that we were both thinking the same thought of how my mother denied ever sleeping with this man, my now biological father. Hold up, she didn't deny it once or twice but three times and my husband and children witnessed it for themselves. I also thought to myself: I defended her and her word at that restaurant, I completely believed her and now I feel betrayed by her. Should I feel betrayed?

As I thought and thought and as we drove further and further I became more and more confused, heart-shooked, and curious as to why my mother would do such a thing to me, her daughter. So, I asked my husband if he didn't mind turning the car around so I could go and visit my mother about this. I really didn't want to take his moment away from him but something said that waiting to speak about it wasn't the right thing to do and that it must be done now. Mind you, I wasn't angry at all, I guess I hadn't reached that point yet and wasn't sure if I was going to get to that level of emotion. I was more or less still in a state of shock. The point of the matter is,

I wanted to know if this guy was my biological father and I found out the official truth. Next I know, I went from being shocked to feeling betrayed and hurt. Things were so puzzling to me and I honestly couldn't wrap my mind around it. Growing up, I just wanted to know who I belong to, my other half, just as my siblings did. Why not I have the same opportunity? What did I do? Really, I thought, "no one has your back like your mother." My Mother. But, whose back did she have, mine or hers? Ughhhhhh!

This is some real sh't man.

My husband and I decided to put our original plans/trip on hold for a few hours in hopes of finding out answers from my mother to this new dilemma.

We had driven so far to where it's now dark outside as we approached the next exit to turn around and change the course of our trip. I told my husband, 'it is what it is, we already have the results, and at this point I just want to know why she had to lie to me'. Mentally

arranging the puzzle pieces. Then I thought, all those

years, I grew up thinking another man was my dad based

upon what she said. Then it dawned to me that my

"now" biological father told me this when I was about

seven years old and I also wondered why would my

mother allow this guy to enter into our home, and come

to my room to talk with me? He wasn't a stranger to her

but he was a stranger to me and my siblings at that time

and she let him come to the room not once but twice. Ok,

what's really going on? I'm so confused and totally

distraught, but I still held it together. I mean, I wanted to

find out the results and I did, so there was nothing else

really to do about it. But, I still felt like I needed to know

why she lied; just WHY?

I know I couldn't go to my mother's house all

hay-wired. Remember, no one else knew this was done

and for the most part I was fine, I was ok, I guess. Before

getting to my mother's house, I decided to call my younger brother. I knew he had a computer in his room and I at least wanted to ask him if I could use it prior to getting there. I didn't want to enter his room without permission even though I am his BIG SISTER. We spoke and he said I could use it and that he was on his way. I told him I would fill him in on what was going on later. I knew the DNA representative had sent the results via my email address and this would be the only way for me to prove the DNA test results to my mother.

As we are approaching my mother's home, I also decided to call my stepdad. For some reason, I felt that he needed to know. I didn't feel I needed to tell him face to face; the root of my problem was my mother, so calling him was good for me. I told him and he was not as shocked as I thought he would be. He stated he always had a hunch that she could possibly be lying about whom she said was my biological father but he had no proof and just went with the story she told him as well as others.

So, we arrive to my mom's house and I was still on the phone with my stepdad. My husband exited the vehicle, walked up the stairs to the porch, to the front door and knocked. My mother opened the door surprised to see us as ever. No one knew we were in town or coming in to town. She was happy for the most part, but she was 'throwed-off'-- confused as to why we were visiting without prior notice. You could tell. I heard her ask my husband where I was and he told her I was still in the car talking to my stepdad. I heard this because I had the car door propped open while I was on the cell phone talking. As she proceeds toward the car, I try to finish up my conversation with my stepdad. I needed to know from him how to come at her to get the information I needed. He said there isn't anything you can do but to simply tell her and ask her what you need to know. My mother then says "hey" and I tell her I was hanging up the phone right now, and that I was coming, so she turns around and proceeds to go back into the house.

Well, I hang up the cell phone with my stepdad, and I enter the house. I gave my mom a hug and a kiss and tell her that I needed to get something from my email. She said ok. I told her that I had already called my brother to use his computer. So she continued on to watch television and my husband and I went to the room to find the email from DNA representative.

You would think his computer would be powered on, but no, I had to power it on and wait for it to boot up. Part four of the nerve wrecking experience. Ok, that was just the anxiousness inside me getting the best of me and my nerves are frantic and everywhere. My husband pretty much stood by my side, subtly awaiting anxiously himself. Took a hot minute to get everything going but I finally got there. I am so rushing to log in to my email because I just have to see the DNA test results with my own two eyes. Here it goes! It's opening up! BAM! There it is. And it reads as so, he's my biological father, 99.9999%. This is CRAZY!

So, I called out to my mother and asked if she could come to the room, that I needed her to read something in my email. She replied "ok" and came to the room. I let her sit down in the chair. Using the computer mouse, I scrolled to the top left of the document and asked her to read the name, and she did. I then scrolled to the top right of the document and asked to her to read the name and she did as well. I then scrolled to the bottom of the document and asked her to read the paragraph and she did. It's funny how she read the names aloud but read the paragraph silently.

To my surprise, my mother ANGRILY stands up, SLAPPED her left thigh with her left hand and THREW her arm/hand up in the air and said to me, "Meh, now you

95

know" and STORMED out of the room. She proceeded to go back to the living room, sit down and continued watching television. Now as she stormed out of the room, I sat down in the chair in disbelief and complete total shock of her actions. My husband stood there in total shock as well.

I said to myself ever so quietly, "did she just say what she said and did what she did?" And I thought, "Did she just totally disregard me? ME, HER DAUGHTER!" I was absolutely throwed-off, surprised, confused, perturb and angry. Seeing her reaction made me feel as if I had just gotten hit and ran over by a Mack truck and landed faced down in mud, heartless. No, it was as if my mother stood there with a smile on her face, took her hand, stuck it in my chest, squeezed my heart with all her might and just watched all the hurt and pain ooze. My heart was crushed. I was clueless as to how to react or what to say. Standing there looking dumbfounded, I think I had an outer body experience. The spiritual me remained standing in the doorway of my brother's room and the physical me stood up, and said "Oh, Hell No!" I want to say, I became angry, I saw angry. As I left the bedroom and proceed to the living room, I can see she is sitting there with her legs crossed while watching television. One of her legs rocked/kicked back and forth nervously. I think she was just as shocked. Not shocked as to whom the father was but shocked as to ME getting a DNA test done and she knew nothing about it or maybe all of the above. So I stood in front of her while she sat there watching television and I said, "Momma, are you serious?", "Really, is that all you have to say?" She replied with, "Meh, now you know".

Although remaining respectable, I went off (I clicked). I reminded her of how she lied to me in front of my husband and my children. I told her that I specifically asked her if she had slept with him and I reminded her of her answers. I told her that I defended her in her absence at the restaurant against her sister and brother-in-law and the mob they brought along with them. I reminded her of all the years I thought another man was my father and how she knew it wasn't true. I told her that I LIVED HER LIE for her. I actually and literally LIVED HER LIE. She watched her lie play out and I was a product of it. All her siblings knew, I was told my own maternal grandmother knew and she took the information to her grave and I spent a lot of time with my maternal grandmother. Still, I was kept in the dark, living out a lie. I asked her if she had planned on taking this to her grave and prayed that I would never find out because she sure wasn't ever going to tell me. I didn't give her time to respond. I was on a rant and rave at this point. I asked her how could she afford my siblings before me and after me to know their fathers and their extended families and hold me captive from mine. WHY? WHAT WAS THE BIG SECRET?

I told her I needed answers and that she owed me at least that much. She replies, she doesn't remember. Even my husband tried to ask her a few questions and she stated she couldn't remember. I huff a bit and say, "Oh you remember, you remember something". All these years, really? I told her that I really wasn't concerned with who my father was and when and where it happened and why it happened. What concerned me was 'why did she lie to me'. Why did she feel or believe it was necessary to lie?

So to find out the reason for the lie, I had to ask questions to try and drill it out of her. She was so reluctant to give me anything and what she gave wasn't as clear as expected. Now she begins to cry, really? While she's crying, I continue to try and get some answers. Let me pause for a second....My mother's tears could have meant that the news she just heard was a shock to her, to now really, truly, and finally hearing the truth from all those years of wondering herself....un-pause....Sorry, I saw right through the crying, those tears had no affect on my emotional state. She tells me the history of the two men and their relevance to her. She provides me with dates of when she encountered each of the two individuals and she told me about each man and what was going on within their lives at that time. She gave me the information but in bits and pieces, so of course, I had to struggle and try to put all of the information together to try and create a clear picture of some sort. And mind you, I didn't get all the answers I needed to make some sense out of it. I received some concrete answers and I received some 'I don't remember' answers.

I told her, my sibling's fathers' weren't perfect, but she allowed my siblings' the opportunity to get to know their fathers and allowed them to make their own decision for their fathers to be a part of their lives. And to top it off, my father only lived a few miles away from me, my entire life. So, it wasn't as if he or I couldn't get to each other. I just don't understand and it is so unfair and so unclear to me. It's so obvious that I cannot change the past, I receive that, but I am trying to find a way to make something of the future. Still trying to piece it all together, still confusing as heck though and I still don't know the BIG SECRET.

I decided that I wasn't really getting anywhere that evening and I told my husband that its best we leave. Just before actually leaving, I informed my mother where we (her and I) now stand amongst each other, that I still have unanswered questions for her, that I will continue to ask, and her choosing not to answer will not deter me from asking. I paused for a moment because I had become emotionally exhausted. I think my spiritual body eventually caught up with me and I just couldn't battle any more with it. Although my heart dwindled as if barely hanging on a piece of string blowing in the wind, I gave my mother a hug, a kiss goodbye, told her that I forgave her and that I love her. It had come to me at that moment that my battle was to find out the truth, my identity and being accountable for her actions and acknowledging the truth was her battle.

I know I will always love and respect my mother, she's my mother and she raised me. To help ease the hurt, the pain and not allow myself to become overwhelmed of the situation, I guess I have to continue to verbally remind myself of that. But, how do I, now at this present time, deal with her as an adult or as a person. I am still trying to put the puzzle pieces together and some things add up and some things don't. I try and give the benefit of the doubt and put my own conclusions together, but it's no good when there is no confirmation on the subject.

A few days have passed, maybe a week or so and I speak to my father. I believe I called him. My personal opinion, I don't think he was too sure what to do at this rate. Seemed to me he got his confirmation and I was somehow still defending my mother cause a part of me didn't want to give him the satisfaction of having an "I told you so" attitude. Just because something he said was proven, I wasn't letting his ass off the hook that easy either. If he knew all this damn time, where were the visits, where was child support, where was the support mentally and emotionally, where was your ass and why you chose not to be around, regardless? Why did you wait until I was grown for you to all of a sudden have some guts...oh wait, you didn't have that either because from what I recall, you let your brother and sister-in-law do you dirty work for you, though you had guts when I was what, seven, a young child. Seriously! Yes, I am ANGRY! He didn't do sh*t for me, not even to stand up for me, fight for me, nor claimed me. Why would you stir things up when I was a young child and then have no guts to fall through with your accusations. He waded in my life like Casper the ghost. And you know what's troubling, he was ok with himself for doing as such. Unacceptable!

Anyway, moving on.

I called and spoke to him and, yes, I asked all those questions. He derailed from answering my questions and got on his own rant about his life and how things were for him in the beginning when all this popped off (happened). His conversations, his thoughts, his words were all over the place as if he was a fly trapped in a jar trying to get out. He was so stuck on himself and about himself that we got nowhere and you know what, that was not what I needed. I was so mad at him; I could have slapped him straight through the phone. I tried to get him to stay focus on the questions I was asking, but he was all over the place, so I decided conversation needed to end. I almost hung up in his face. He stated he would stay in touch and I replied "yeah, we'll see". I told him based upon where we are in this so called father-daughter relationship; actions speak louder than words at this moment in time. That was the second conversation held.

I then went to my husband and informed him that the conversation I had with my father didn't get anywhere; although, I was able to put some of his pieces with some of the pieces of information I received from my mother to make an understanding of a few things. My parents are both difficult when trying to retrieve information, but I sure as heck was not giving up on trying. I want to know, wouldn't you?

I believe months have passed and no phone calls. My father stated that I didn't have to worry about a thing; he was going to make the effort. It's not as if I really needed him to call; I thought we could make the situation a positive one, a new relationship of some kind, healing of some sort. It also had to do with him keeping his word and I tried to give him the benefit of the doubt, but that was shot to death. My husband felt he needed to step in the situation based upon what my father stated among the conversation they had, and decided to contact my father to find out what's going on. I think my husband became frustrated that a man alive and well not doing right by his word and as a man, period. I also believe my husband was worried that this would take some affect on me and I would act it out negatively towards him and our kids or even myself. From what I remember, he calls up my father and they have a discussion. My husband stated he asked my father why it took him that long to say anything and if he knew the truth all those years, why wasn't he there? My father blamed my mother and stated that she told him to stay away and to not say anything. My father's justification was that he told his family, but his family had better not repeat it. Clearly, that was not justification at all. All those years they had a hunch but didn't say anything. For the most part, I guess it's true as the saying goes, 'Momma's baby, and Poppa's maybe'. I can only assume his family's point of view was why bother with the situation. My opinion, it was just something else for them to talk about, needless to say, pushing the issue at all; gossip I guess. My husband shared his views about the whole situation to my father. I appreciated my husband for doing that, because that lets my father know I have support. My husband, as well as I, didn't gain much from the conversation he and my father had. Today, I am still in the same position with getting my questions answered--nowhere. It just seems that neither of my parents want to take responsibility for their actions (and they haven't) thus avoiding me to avoid me bringing up the subject.

My maternal grandmother used to always tell me to keep my mouth shut, my eyes open and to observe. Didn't know I had to be of discern with my own family. Overall, growing up, I felt a bit as if I were an outsider and at times I felt lost. To this day, being knowledgeable of the information I now have, I honestly feel as if I do not belong. I attribute this feeling to the fact that my father didn't fight for me as if I was his own as he did his other children and my mother sure didn't do as much to help make the situation a positive one even though in her mind all things remained positive as long as she was able to control the situation (I assume). I had been in the dark for so long and had the wool pulled over my eyes to when I came about of the truth, I didn't know what to believe nor did I know how I should exactly feel. And upon discovering the truth and at that moment, I was angry (lived someone else's lie), confused (my truth and identity wasn't true), hurt (what I thought I loved and knew was taken away from me), ashamed and embarrassed (I spent my life chasing emptiness while others, who knew the truth, watched), helpless (I couldn't change the real truth or the past), awkward (lost within my mental state), I felt betrayed (lied to by my own mother) as well as disassociated from my maternal family just as I felt disassociated with my paternal family and I didn't know if my feelings were valid. Was I entitled? Would knowing my paternal family, needless to say my father, make a difference in the development of the person I am today? There really is no way of knowing now. To be honest with you, although we are biologically connected there is no bond that seals it. Let's just say, I came to terms a long time ago that I would never have that "feeling of being daddy's little girl". It's a shame that a father-daughter relationship is a waste. All I can say is "out of sight, out of mind". Don't get me wrong, I want to be mad, I want to be angry and I want to hold a grudge, so deep, it'll cut below their feet. Trust me, I really want to be bitter and mean towards my mother, towards my father, towards my aunts and uncles, heck, towards anyone who knew. I deserve to have a moment, right? What prevents me from doing so is reflecting on how *God* has blessed me so much. I wouldn't benefit from being negative and to do so is not worth my time and energy. It is a good thing, no, it is a great thing, that *there is a God.* For all who have endured some of life's discomfort whether it be minor or major, give *God* the praise. Because it is those discomforts that teach (if you learn from them) the lessons that shape and mold each of us today. There is still a good life to live when it is all said and done. I can honestly and truthfully say I, my life, is and has been *blessed.* As I reflect on events that took place during my childhood thus leading to where I am now as an adult, I have no choice but to believe *God* covered me, held me, ordered my steps and governed my path. In my heart, I believe LOVE, true LOVE, stemmed the secrets, the sheltering, the deprivation of their truth and the deprivation of my identity. Everyone had their justifiable reasons for doing as they felt. The question that still remain is, "what is the big secret that kept me deprived of the truth and of my identity?".........I am still trying to discover that.

This book was not written as a sign of detestation or exploitation, but as a means of healing. I hope Deprived Truth, Deprived Identity offer a way of giving hope, prompt those who deal with life's discomforts to look within themselves and discover their peace as well as recognize that life is still good. By *God* and through *God*, you, as I, will prevail.

About the Author.... Mignon V. Walker is originally from Lafayette, Louisiana and currently resides in Converse, Texas. A military veteran of the U.S. Air Force, she has earned three collegiate degrees, numerous accolades and is an active volunteer within her community. Mignon continues to motivate herself and others to strive to be superlative as she is an advocate of personal growth and development: spiritually, physically, emotionally and mentally. She enjoys poetry, traveling, spending time with her family, music, modeling, comedy, watching sports and motivating others (not in that particular order). This is her first published book.

Mignon Valliere Walker

www.ingramcontent.com/pod-product-compliance
Lightning Source LLC
Chambersburg PA
CBHW072149020426
42334CB00018B/1929